Tweenies™

CBeebies BBC

wheels, wings and whirly things

look book

The Tweenies love trucks and trains, boats and bulldozers, and cars and cranes. They like to look at different things that float and fly, rumble and rock, and sail and soar.

They **love** looking at wheels, wings and whirly things.

telly time

Milo loves the big, noisy machines on building sites. Join Milo, as Max shows him a video all about diggers, cranes and other very noisy things.

Word time

- digger
- crane
- bulldozer
- drill
- cement mixer
- dumper truck
- wheel barrow
- tractor

Machine-a-rooney! Milo thinks that the building site is really cool. The site's foreman is showing Max and Milo around. They wear hard hats to protect their heads, good hard boots and bright yellow jackets so they can be seen easily.

roller

digger

steering wheel

tyre

caterpillar tracks

piston

radiator

scoop

spade

lamp

pipes

telly time

Fizz likes cars, buses and trucks. Judy shows her a video all about vehicles. The video shows a busy scene in a town.

Word time

- caravan
- truck
- motorbike
- jeep
- trailer
- tanker
- bus

Fizz and Judy have driven
to the motorway. They
stop at a service station
to look out over the big
road. There are so many
things to see. Fizz likes to
count the cars.

bus

petrol cap

caravan

tow bar

exhaust pipe

headlight

Fresh bread

wheel

bonnet

CAR 1

bumper

number plate

Make your own bulldozer

Because Milo and Fizz both like machines with big wheels and tracks, Max shows them how to make their own bulldozers.

You will need:-

apron

corrugated and plain card

toilet roll tubes

glue

empty boxes or margarine tubs

round-ended scissors

sticky tape

paints and brushes

1) To make the caterpillar track, cut the corrugated card into a strip 12cm x 40cm. Join the two ends together with sticky tape to make a band.

   Take two toilet roll tubes and place one at each end of the band. Stick them in place with tape.

2) Glue the box or tub on top of the caterpillar track to make the cab.

3) Tape two pieces of plain card, each 5cm x 15cm, to either side of the cardboard box or tub.

Crease a fold in a piece of plain card, 20cm x 8cm, to make the scoop. Tape it to the front of the bulldozer.

4) Paint and decorate your bulldozer, just like Milo and Fizz are doing.

telly time

Bella loves machines that fly. Max shows her a video about an airshow.

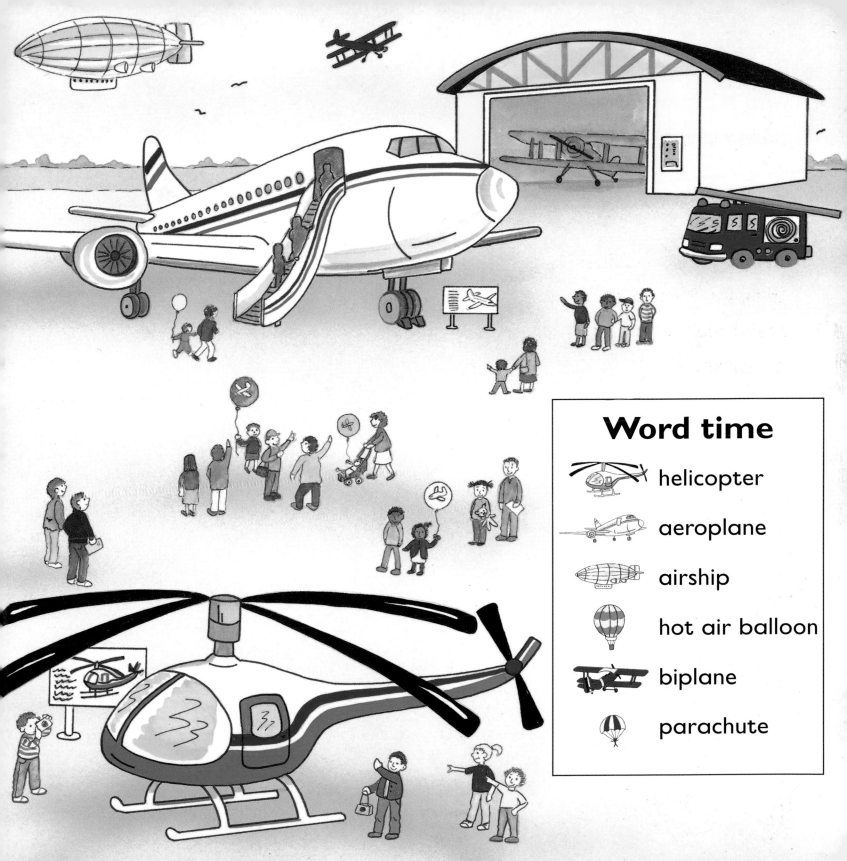

Word time

- helicopter
- aeroplane
- airship
- hot air balloon
- biplane
- parachute

Bella visits a busy airport with Max. An airport guide shows them around.

control tower

fire engine

baggage cart

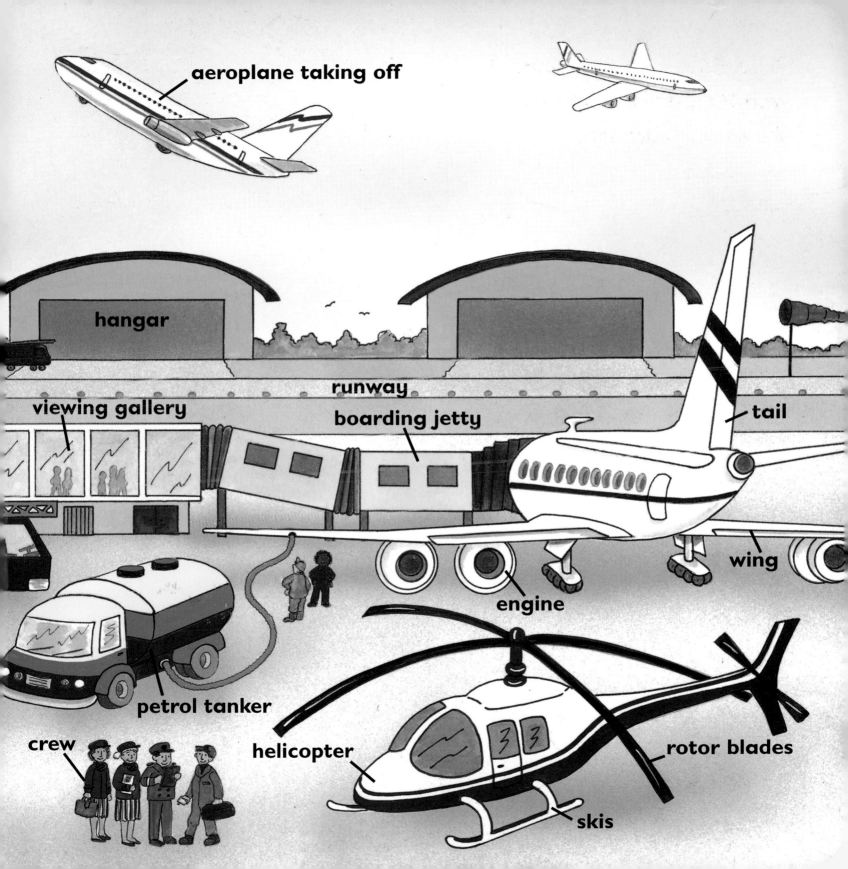

aeroplane taking off

hangar

runway

viewing gallery

boarding jetty

tail

engine

wing

petrol tanker

crew

helicopter

rotor blades

skis

telly time

Jake loves anything that floats, so Judy shows him a video about boats.

Word time

ferry

submarine

fishing boat

sailing boat

lighthouse

catamaran

Judy takes Jake to see the boats and ships in the harbour. The harbour master shows them around.

lobster pots

funnel

life boats

tug boat

liner

fishing boat

anchor

bollard

life belt

Make your own sailing boat

messy time

When Jake gets back to the playgroup, he tells Bella all about the boats. She shows him how to make a sailing boat.

You will need:-

apron

large margarine tub

pencil

lump of modelling clay

piece of card cut into the shape of a triangle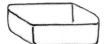

crayons, paints and brushes

sticky tape

1) Push a piece modelling clay into the bottom of the margarine tub. Be sure the clay is in the middle of the tub.

2) Carefully push the point of the pencil into the clay so that it stands upright.

3) Use paints to decorate your card triangle sail.

4) Tape the sail to the pencil mast.

5) Float your boat and sing a song.

Row, row, row your boat,
Gently down the stream.
Merrily, merrily, merrily, merrily,
Life is such a dream!

The Tweenies had a wonderful time with wheels, wings and whirly things. They learned names and made bulldozers and sailing boats, too. What a busy time!